A Gif

D1541442

To: Lewis

From: Joanie Organ Coolidge

Date: 10-16-01

Dear Lew - in thanksgiving for
loaning us Clarke in all
her giftedness as a mother
+ organizer extraordinaire
(see pg 13) May God bless you
richly for your generosity.
With deep gratitude ♡Joanie

Fathering

Building the New Civilization of Love

Stories and Prayers by

Christopher de Vinck

Compiled by

Rosalie McPhee

Cover painting by Michael O'Brien

Design by Rob Huston

First Printing, September 8th, 2000
Feast of the Birth of Mary, Mother of God

Printed in Canada

MADONNA HOUSE PUBLICATIONS
COMBERMERE • ONTARIO • CANADA • K0J 1L0

www.madonnahouse.org

To all fathers,

*That they may know
the hidden fruits of their labor*

The Little Mandate

Arise—go! Sell all you possess. Give it directly, personally to the poor.

Take up My cross (their cross) and follow Me... going to the poor... being poor... being one with them... one with me.

Little, be always little! Be simple... poor... childlike.

Preach the gospel *with your life*, without compromise! Listen to the Spirit, He will lead you.

Do little things exceedingly well for love of Me.

Love... love... love... never counting the cost.

Go into the marketplace and stay with Me. Pray... fast... pray always... fast.

Be hidden. Be a light to your neighbor's feet. Go without fears into the depth of men's hearts. I shall be with you.

Pray always. I will be your rest.

The Little Mandate was given to Catherine Doherty from the Holy Spirit as she listened intently to hear how God wanted her to live the Gospel. Many others have heard the echo of these words in their own hearts and also endeavor to live them.

Table of Contents

Introduction

Many fathers seem to be in the business of serving their children. They change their diapers, buy them shoes, drive them to proms and baseball games, advise them, cherish them, sing to them at night, pray with them. On the other hand, some fathers are incapable of doing anything for their children.

There are fathers who are able to embrace their families, and some fathers who have no relationships with their sons and daughters. This little book is for all fathers, for those who know how to love their children, and for those who do not.

When Christ was asked how we are to live, he said that he wanted people to love each other. I never fully understood his desire until all three of our children were born. Now I know what it is that I wish for when I die. I wish to know that David, Karen, and Michael love each other. I cannot explain exactly why that is so, but as a father, it is very important for me to know that my children embrace one another in awe. I suppose it is because I see the extraordinary gifts that these three children hold within themselves.

If someone were to ask me which of my children I love the best, I would not be able to answer that—for each one in my eyes is holy, extraordinary, bright, funny, good, brave, kind.

If we could love one another as a father loves his children, we would have a dramatically different world. A father sees through a child's flaws. A father sees the inner nature of a son or daughter, that inside, hidden part, that soul part, and when a father sees the soul part of the child, he sees hints of God's work, and whenever we see hints of God's work, a deep sense of love is triggered deep within ourselves.

Many fathers, when they see their children, gasp with joy and gratitude. Perhaps this is how God feels when he thinks of us. This is how I feel when I think of my three children, and I want to pass along that feeling to them.

Catherine Doherty had a special respect and love for priests, the fathers of our church. She recognized the power of the paternal embrace. To be accepted and loved under the care of the father connects us with a spiritual self, allows us to claim a self-worth, a self-love which then can be given to others freely and with confidence.

Many priests have the insight and compassion and love to tell people that they are loved, that they are good, that God deeply loves them. Such spiritual affirmation brings great sustenance to people. It is the same sustenance that a father brings to his sons and daughters. To say to his children that he is proud of them, that they are good, that they are pretty, that they are brave, that they are compassionate, that they are merciful, that they are humble…such affirmation brought to the children from the fathers protects the children as they move into the world that is often not compassionate and affirming.

Be inspired by this small book of meditations, oh you fathers of faith and goodness. Your children are waiting for you to serve them.

Christopher de Vinck

Source of All Fatherhood

I bow my knees before the Father, from whom every family in heaven and on earth is named, that according to the riches of his glory he may grant you to be strengthened with might through his Spirit in the inner man, and that Christ may dwell in your hearts through faith; that you, being rooted and grounded in love, may have power to comprehend with all the saints what is the breadth and length and height and depth, and to know the love of Christ which surpasses knowledge, that you may be filled with all the fullness of God.

Ephesians 3: 14-19

When I was a boy, I raised a newborn squirrel I found on the ground at the base of a large tree. I saved a skunk from being killed on the road, and once when I was six I kept a butterfly in a box during a rainstorm because I was afraid it would drown.

During the last few weeks of Roe's pregnancy with our first son, I had a great fear. My mother and I were sitting in her sunny kitchen. "Mom, I am very worried about something," I said with a low, serious voice.

"Yes?" my mother said as she leaned a bit closer to me from across the kitchen table.

"Well, you know how much I love animals?"

"What is it, Chris?" my mother asked. "Tell me."

"Well…when the baby is born, will I love him or her as much as I loved those animals when I was a child?"

My mother looked at me, leaned back in her chair, and then she just began to laugh in a fit of delight and amusement. "You have no idea what it is like to love your own child. Of course you don't know this because you have never been a father." Then she laughed some more. "Christopher, when

7

the baby is born, you will be amazed at how much love you will give and feel. Don't worry. We human beings are built to love. There is a place in our hearts to love animals, and art and music…and there is a place to love our children. That place in your heart is empty at the moment because your child has not yet been born."

David was born three weeks later, and when the nurse wrapped him in a blanket, I asked if I could hold him, and the nurse laughed, "Of course you can hold him. You are his father."

That was the first time someone called me a father. I was a father. I knew that David would be a part of me for the rest of my life. I loved him more than the geese and mice and turtles, and I laughed to myself when I thought about the conversation I had with my mother three weeks earlier.

The father loves his children. I knew, for the first time, what God might feel towards his children. The source of fatherhood is love. The source of love is God. God the Father. God of love. It is easy to know God's will if you are blessed to be a father.

God, dear brothers, in a sense shares his father-hood with each of you. Not in the mysterious and supernatural way in which he did with Joseph of Nazareth...And yet every fatherhood on earth, every human fatherhood takes its beginning from God, and finds its model in Him.

Pope John Paul II, Homily, March 19, 1981

A father must be strong enough to allow the rest of the family to lean on him. Since God the Father is love, mercy and tenderness, so man must possess these virtues in a great measure. His very virility is always expressed in that love, that tenderness, that mercy and that understanding.

Catherine Doherty, Dearly Beloved Vol. I

Joseph in his turn, in the home in Nazareth, offered the child who was growing beside him the support of his well-balanced virility, his far-sightedness, his courage, his gifts which every good father has, deriving them from that supreme source "from whom every family in heaven and on earth takes its name." (Ephesians 3:15)

Pope John Paul II, Homily, March 19, 1981

Do not look forward to what may happen tomorrow. The same Eternal Father who cares for you today will care for you tomorrow and every day of your life. He will either shield you from suffering, or he will give you unfailing strength to bear it. Be at peace then, and put aside all anxious thoughts.

St. Francis de Sales

The bowl of the sea holds water. The valley collects rich soil. A tree is held by its roots. And a child is held by the father. God of all children, help me cup my babies like hands under the sea; help me embrace my daughter as the valley embraces; let me be, oh God, wet roots so that my children may grow toward your holy name, name of the Father, name of the Son, name of the Holy Spirit. We grow strong in the embrace of the Father, that tree, that valley, that sea.

Listen to the Spirit. He will lead you.

The Little Mandate

Co-creator
with the Father

God created man in his own image, in the image of
God he created him; male and female he created
them. And God blessed them, and God said to
them, "Be fruitful and multiply, and fill the earth
and subdue it."

Genesis 1: 27-28

*T*he doctor looked up at me during the last moments of Roe's second pregnancy. The baby was in distress, and not moving. Its head was visible, but nothing happened. Then the doctor said to me, "Chris, push just here, on this lower portion of Roe's abdomen while I pull on the baby's head and shoulders."

Roe pushed. I pushed. The doctor pulled, and our daughter, Karen, was born. She was blue, and the umbilical cord was wrapped around her neck. The doctor quickly clipped and snipped; the baby was hurriedly taken out of the birthing room. Roe and I were silent. I said a prayer to Mary that the baby be protected. Moments later, a pink, screaming little girl was returned, and within seconds she was nursing at her mother's full breast.

I knew then that I would always be with Karen, pushing her forward into life, and praying for her health. It seems to me that is what a father does: provide and protect life. I knew during my first years as a father that I could not handle such responsibilities alone, but with Roe, with doctors and teachers and brothers and sisters I could be a provider, be a model, be a father, and celebrate God in my daughter.

Sometimes when Karen is being difficult about an issue I say, "You were just as stubborn when you were born," and Karen smiles, and I smile too.

What God does for the universe man does for his human family. God provides for eternity; man for a short space of time. Therefore man expresses the will of the Father by being a father. To be a father, he must be a creator and provider.

Catherine Doherty, Dearly Beloved Vol. I

Children should be loved for the love of Him who created them, and not for the love of self nor of the children.

St. Catherine of Siena

For the "civilization of love" it is essential that the husband should recognize that the motherhood of his wife is a gift: this is enormously important for the entire process of raising children. Much will depend on his willingness to take his own part in this first stage of the gift of humanity, and to become willingly involved as a husband and father in the motherhood of his wife.

Pope John Paul II, Letter to Families

13

Joined in marriage, man and woman reflect God's image and are in a certain way the "revelation" of His love: not only of the love that God cherishes for human beings, but also of that mysterious communion which characterizes the inner life of the three divine Persons. Childbirth itself, which makes every family a sanctuary of life, can also be considered an image of God. The Apostle Paul tells us that all fatherhood and motherhood derive from God. He is the ultimate source of life. It can therefore be stated that every person's genealogy is rooted in the eternal. In conceiving a child, parents are acting as God's co-workers.

Pope John Paul II, Angelus Message, February 6th, 1994

Give me the wisdom, oh Father, to watch my children in silence, to teach them by my example, to push them forward when they need to be pushed, and to call upon you when they are in need.

Love... love... love... never counting the cost.

The Little Mandate

Protector
and Guardian

An angel of the Lord appeared to Joseph in a dream and said, "Rise, take the child and his mother, and flee to Egypt, and remain there till I tell you; for Herod is about to search for the child, to destroy him." And he rose and took the child and his mother by night, and departed to Egypt, and remained there until the death of Herod.

Matthew 2:13-14

*M*y father wrote books, taught French and philosophy in various colleges and universities, was a lawyer, an editor, a tennis player, a weaver, and he was also a carpenter. Perhaps he liked to work with wood above all his avocations. He built wood castles for my brothers and me, wood swords, and weaving looms, but above all else, my father built full-sized wooden sailboats and, as he was always proud to say, without using any power tools.

For many evenings when I was a boy, I sat at my father's side and watched him cut wood, sand it, shape it, bend it. As he worked he told me about the days he sailed on the lakes in Belgium as a young man.

I liked to watch his long hands grasp a file and chisel a piece of wood into a handle or keel or paddle. I liked the smell of the wood glue he used. I liked to watch him twist the screwdriver a final turn as the screw was tightly secure deep inside the giving wood.

My father liked to build things. He didn't talk much. He was devoted to my mother. They were married for fifty-five years. He went to work each day. I never heard him complain. He was a father to six children, one of whom was severely handi-

capped, blind, incapable of learning or hearing, or walking. My father shaped his family with the chisel of his heart, creating a home of peace, a place that was held together with the glue of his heart.

When I think of my father, I often think about the young man sailing on his wooden sailboats in Belgium, and I think of the old, old man sitting in the living room reading. My father was born the year the Titanic sank. In my life, in my heart, his little boat is sailing still, having overcome the icebergs of life, having carried his family safely to the continent of confidence and goodness.

My father was a carpenter. He knew how to build a boat and a family. He will always protect me with the memory of those evenings we spent together in the basement as we both listened to the scratch, scratch, scratching sound of the sandpaper rubbing against the rough and ready wood.

The family, even as the individual, must "know God through love, in order to reach him." But love has for a footstool humility and simplicity. Let the family go to Joseph, the carpenter of Nazareth, and ask him to make them into such footstools, for well does that holy carpenter know these two.

Skillfully his strong hands will do the work, and easily will he bring the family these two virtues, because he knows that if they possess them, they will possess God, his foster Son.

Catherine Doherty, Dear Parents

Where, dear fathers, will you be able to draw the energy necessary to assume in various circumstances the right attitude that your children, even without knowing it, expect from you? Saint Joseph offers you the answer to this: it is in God, the source of all fatherhood, it is in his way of acting with men, which is revealed to us by Sacred Scripture, that you can find the model of a fatherhood capable of making a positive impression on the educational process of your children, not smothering their spontaneity on the one hand, nor abandoning their still immature personality to the traumatizing experiences of insecurity and loneliness on the other.

Pope John Paul II, Homily, March 19, 1981

Above all, where social and cultural conditions so easily encourage a father to be less concerned with his family or at any rate less involved in the work of education, efforts must be made to restore socially the conviction that the place and task of the father in and for the family is of unique and irreplaceable importance.

Pope John Paul II,
The Role of the Christian Family in The Modern World

Like God the Father, he is the protector, the final authority, and the head of the family.

Catherine Doherty, Dearly Beloved Vol. I

I pray for them. I do not pray for the world but for the ones you have given me, because they are yours.

John 17:9

Christian husband! Imitate St. Joseph by beginning your day's work with God, and ending it for Him. Cherish those belonging to you as the holy foster father did Jesus, and be their faithful protector.

St. John Vianney

In the name of the Father, always in the name of the Father, let us pray in the name of the Father. Let us bow down with the Father's name on our lips. Let us imitate the Father as he works in silence, tending to the garden, the workshop, the labor of his will. We are your children, Lord, under your protection and guidance. We say your name when we are alone or when we are among our friends. In your name we celebrate our labor, we celebrate your love. In the name of you, Father, we pray. Watch over us. Protect us. With your name on our lips and in our hearts, with your name we pray for your presence among us this day.

Love... love... love... never counting the cost.

The Little Mandate

Toil of Love

Therefore, my beloved brethren, be steadfast, immovable, always abounding in the work of the Lord, knowing that in the Lord your labor is not in vain.

I Corinthians 15: 58

I am a school administrator in the largest high school in New Jersey, which encompasses four large buildings which could all stand alone as separate schools. During a typical work week I must walk thirty miles throughout the halls meeting with teachers and administrators, delivering books and messages, seeking out guidance counselors and students.

Sometimes, when I am very tired, and I receive a call in my office from a teacher four buildings away who wants to see me, I start my long walk. I think about the routine of my job, the 24 years I have been working, the worn tires on my car, the pile of paper work on my desk. I sometimes just want to walk out of the building and leave the job, the family, the burdens and, well, just go off and seek pleasure and wealth and peace, but then I make a little chant in my head as I walk: "Each step helps pay for college. Each step helps pay for college."

My oldest son is in graduate school, my youngest daughter is a freshman in college, and Michael, the youngest son will be in college in a year. I, like many fathers, have worked for years to pay the bills, to buy a house, to provide food and clothing for my wife and children, and now I am paying college bills.

But when I come home to my family in the tired evening, I see all the pleasure and wealth and peace all men seek.

When man works to provide for his family's subsistence, that means that he puts all the daily toil of his love into his work. For it is love that brings the family into being, it is love that is its constant expression, its stable environment.

Pope John Paul II, Homily, May 31, 1980

Subdue the earth! This role Saint Joseph recognized and accepted in life, transmitting to the young Jesus who was growing at his side the spirit of joyful readiness with which he resumed his daily task every morning.

Pope John Paul II, Homily, March 19, 1983

Consider for a moment the situation of the father of a family. He works hard for this family to fulfill their needs. At times he dreams of greener fields opening up for him. However, if he loves his family he will not follow those dreams if they conflict with the real needs of his loved ones. As monotonous, unsatisfying and painful as this may be, loving fathers demonstrate their responsiveness to the needs of others by sticking to the task at hand.

Catherine Doherty, Dear Father

Work...is not something that people do for the sole purpose of earning a living; it is a human dimension that can and must be sanctified, in order to bring people to the total fulfillment of their vocation as creatures made in the image and likeness of God.

Pope John Paul II, Homily, May 8, 1988

May the favor of the Lord our God be ours. Prosper the work of our hands! Prosper the work of our hands!

Psalm 90: 17

Work...cannot destroy the family. On the contrary, it must unite it, and help to strengthen it. Let the family not become, because of work, a superficial meeting of human beings, a hotel used only for meals and rest!

Pope John Paul II, Angelus, October 25, 1981

Teach us, good Lord, to serve You as You deserve; to give and not to count the cost; to fight and not to heed the wounds; to toil and not to seek for rest; to labor and not to ask for any reward, save that of knowing that we do Your will.

St. Ignatius of Loyola

Help me Lord to maintain the vision of your place, your Heaven and peace, your home of salvation. Help me stay on the path so that I may return each day to your embrace. Though I may sometimes wish to stray, though I sometimes may wish to give up, though I sometimes may stumble, when I look up I know you will be there, my Father, my protector.

Do little things exceedingly well for love of Me.

The Little Mandate

Provider in Simplicity

Listen, my beloved brethren. Has not God chosen those who are poor in the world to be rich in faith and heirs of the kingdom which he has promised to those who love him?

James 2: 5

*D*uring the first weeks of my parents' marriage, my father came home with his first paycheck. He was delighted to have earned a decent wage, and was now ready to buy a beautiful, antique tapestry. When he arrived home and announced to my mother that he was on his way to buy the expensive wall hanging, my mother grabbed an umbrella and clanked my father on the head and said how foolish, how unwise, how much in need they were of food and shoes. Ever since that time, my mother handled the finances in the house where I grew up.

When Roe and I married, when we returned from our honeymoon, I was now ready to buy the oak dining room table and the matching oak chairs for our little two bedroom house. Roe looked at me as if she was ready to grab an umbrella. "Chris," she said, "the dinette set from my college days is good enough." "Yeah," I answered, "but it looks so cheap." Roe said, with hurt in her voice, that that was the table and chairs from her own home when she was growing up. We kept that set for twenty years.

When I sold my first book to Doubleday, I bought Roe that oak dining room set. She was pleased and charmed, but reminded me that the table and chairs *came after many, many years of writing and working and laughing and praying.*

I have been to the palace in Versailles, I've visited the Vanderbilt mansions and the Morgans' city homes, but each time I sit for a meal at our oak dining room table, this is where I feel like a king and tycoon. My father was crowned with an umbrella and he never bought himself anything that I can remember except bits of wood for his sailboats. I was crowned with the jewels of my wife and children. I have said all along that these are my priorities: God, Roe, the children, and my writing.

Very often I ask the students at school what they want in the future, and again and again they say wealth and fame. I suggest that if we learn to seek the simplicity of material things, we may have extra time to seek the richness of spiritual things: the fortune of God's love, and the fame among God's people.

Go to Joseph…the poor man whose foster Son was born in a stable and whose family lived most frugally in a little forgotten village of Palestine but who held in his arms the wealth of the nations and the Light of the world and who can teach us all how to empty our hands of tinsel and fill them with love, faith, and happiness.

Catherine Doherty, Grace in Every Season

"Fight hunger by changing your lifestyle" is a motto which has appeared in Church circles and which shows the people of the rich nations how to become brothers and sisters of the poor. We need to turn to a more austere way of life which will favor a new model of development that gives attention to ethical and religious values.

Pope John Paul II, The Mission of the Redeemer

Consider the fathers, whose goal is wealth, success, social standing and recognition, the endless keeping up with the Joneses, and anything and everything else but the primary needs of the family. Here, right here, the nature of man and woman are confused, the tranquility of God's wondrous order is broken. Is it a wonder, then, that children can't get answers to their unspoken questions in the one book they can read before their infant eyes can absorb the light of the sun— the book of parental harmony, mutual love, and the constant example of peaceful following of God's design for their family?

Catherine Doherty, Dear Parents

The love of worldly possessions is a sort of bird-lime, which entangles the soul, and prevents it flying to God.

St. Augustine

All over the Western world, men and women are trying to dispossess themselves of their many goods and possessions in order to follow their visions. It appears that the modern conscience cannot stand anymore the disparity between the rich and poor.

Catherine Doherty, Grace in Every Season

God, grant that I my see the jewels of your love, the gold of your heart, the money of your soul. Though I am thirsty, only water from your well will quench me. Though I may seek castles, only your house will keep me warm. Though I may desire caviar and champagne, only your bread will satisfy my hunger.

Blessed are the sounds of your voice for it has more music than all the symphonies in the world. Blessed are the words you have given us for they are more famous than England's Shakespeare, America's Whitman, and Africa's songs. Blessed are your crown of thorns for they signify more authority than diamonds and rubies and sapphires. Help me choose, Father, what is simple and wise, and pure, and gentle so that I may see what is truly rich and valuable.

Arise—go! Sell all you possess.
Give it directly, personally to the poor.

The Little Mandate

Teacher and Guide

Train up a child in the way he should go, and when he is old he will not depart from it.

Proverbs 22:

*T*here is a photograph in our family album of my son David and me raking the leaves in front of the house many years ago. What makes this picture charming are the similarities. I was wearing sneakers and white socks. David wanted to wear his sneakers and white socks too. I was holding the rake in my two hands. David was holding his little bamboo rake in his two hands, just like his dad did. He was wearing a white t-shirt. So was I. David imitated much of what I did when he was a child: shaving with his little boy plastic razor, crossing his legs on the coffee table just like his father, tossing pebbles in the lake just like I did.

Today David is twenty years old. The other day he and his friend, Oana, joined my wife Roe and me for lunch. As we sat at the table, I looked over at the young woman and at the young man. I looked over at Roe, and I knew, once again, that my little boy was imitating his father, choosing to love a woman of intellect and grace and goodness and who possessed a purity of heart.

I still have that little bamboo rake in the shed, and it leans against my big rake, happy souvenirs of a time when the habits of fatherhood rooted and *grounded a child so that he could someday please the father with evidence of a holy future.*

By example, a father preaches his loudest sermons and teaches his greatest lessons. It is from his own tender, responsible actions that his children learn the heart and the art of loving.

Catherine Doherty, Dear Father

A great role, this role of fatherhood, which not a few parents today have tried to abdicate, opting for a relationship on a par with their children, which ends up depriving the children of that psychological support and that moral backing which they need to successfully get through the precarious stage of childhood and early adolescence.

Pope John Paul II, Homily, March 19, 1983

In revealing and in reliving on earth the very fatherhood of God, a man is called upon to ensure the harmonious and united development of all the members of the family: he will perform this task by exercising generous responsibility for the life conceived under the heart of the mother, by a more solicitous commitment to education, a task he shares with his wife, by work which is never a cause of division in the family but promotes its unity and stability, and by means of the witness he gives of an adult Christian life which effectively introduces the children into the living experience of Christ and the Church.

Pope John Paul II,
The Role of the Christian Family in The Modern World

Good example is the most efficacious apostolate. You must be as lighted lanterns and shine like brilliant chandeliers among men. By your example and your words, animate others to know and love God.

St. Mary Joseph Rossello

Father of love, Father of the angels and saints, Father of all who have been born and all who will be born and all who have died and of all who will rise again, I give you thanks for your guidance; I give you thanks for your embrace; I give you thanks for your promise to bring me home to your house. Let me

have the courage to follow your example, the strength to know your will. Let me sit at your table and please you with my day's work. Here I am, Father.

Preach the Gospel *with your life,* without compromise! Listen to the Spirit. He will lead you.

The Little Mandate

The Father's Sacrifice

Then Jesus told his disciples, "If any man would come after me, let him deny himself and take up his cross and follow me. For whoever would save his life will lose it, and whoever loses his life for my sake will find it."

Matthew 16: 24-25

*M*any years ago I asked my father how was it possible that he was able to tend to my brother Oliver for 32 years. "How were you able to carry him for so long, feed him, bath him, work with him all those years?"

My father looked at me and said, "It was not 32 years, Chris. It was simply one day at a time. Can I feed Oliver today? Yes. Can I bath Oliver today? Yes. Can I carry Oliver to a blanket in the sun on the grass today? Yes."

Within a few months after Oliver was born, my parents and the doctors recognized that the baby was not progressing physically or intellectually. Eventually it became clear that Oliver would never see, walk, talk, or think. He sustained such severe brain damage before he was born that Oliver would be confined to a bed all his life.

Over the many years, I watched my father carry Oliver to the bathtub. I watched him shave Oliver and feed Oliver and cut Oliver's hair. My father built Oliver's bed and his diaper box. I watched how my father would lift Oliver's head and place a glass of cold milk to his lips. "See, Chris, just place the glass here and he will drink." And Oliver drank.

It is a struggle to be a father, even when the chidren are healthy. While the rewards are great, the labor sometimes seems insurmountable. We, as fathers, do indeed reap what we sow, but in the sowing there is labor and if such labor can be carried out in love and consistency, the harvest will be rich and sweet.

Oliver didn't look rich and sweet at the beginning of his life. He looked like a mess: twisted legs, blind eyes, no intellect, and yet my father loved Oliver, and worked for his comfort and protection and health. You see, Oliver might have been a physical wreck, but he was not a spiritual wreck. My father knew this. He knew that Oliver's soul was whole and pure and filled with God's presence.

Oliver was a cross my father had to carry, and the only way he was able to carry that burden was to love the burden, to love the cross, to love the boy one day at a time.

The Nobel Prize winning author, Pearl Buck, wrote about her own severely disabled daughter, "There must be acceptance and the knowledge that sorrow fully accepted brings its own gifts. For there is an alchemy in sorrow. It can be transmuted into wisdom, which, if it does not bring joy, can yet bring happiness."

I pick up today's exhaustion and ask myself, can I love my children tomorrow? The answer will always be "Yes I can."

Let husbands place themselves under the patronage of St. Peter. He will teach them how to love through all the storms of the sea of life. He will teach them how to weep when they, in their frailty, will fail and fall. He will impart to them the secret of God's grace and mercy, and tell them how it heals and makes whole again, and gives evermore strength for the immense natural and supernatural task of protecting, cherishing, nourishing and lifting up the 'Little Church', the family entrusted to them.

Catherine Doherty, Dear Parents

Jesus' mission is expressed in the language of love. Indeed, the Sacrifice of the Cross is wholly wrapped in love; and from love it draws its most profound meaning.

John Paul II, Homily, September 14, 1986

We are afraid to love gloriously, joyously, in complete surrender, perhaps because we dimly realize that love is synonymous with sacrifice. And we do not want to have anything to do with sacrifice, which means self-denial, discipline, and submission to authority.

Catherine Doherty, Grace in Every Season

The suffering of adversity does not degrade you but exalts you. The more we are afflicted in this world, the greater is our assurance for the next. The more we sorrow in the present, the greater will be our joy in the future.

St. Isidore of Seville

He who suffers in patience, suffers less and saves his soul. He who suffers impatiently, suffers more and loses his soul.

St. Alphonsus

You have given me the tools, my Father, to build, plow, harvest, create, carry, and bake. You have given me, my Father, the tools to love, pray, heal,

comfort, and teach. Now I pray that you give me the strength to work my hands according to your will, to pull my weight in your name, and to shoulder my cross beside you. Help me build, oh Father, my love for my children one day at a time, and in so doing to build my love for you.

Take up My cross (their cross) and follow me...
going to the poor... being poor...
being one with them... one with Me.

The Little Mandate

Servant-Giver

I was hungry and you gave me food, I was thirsty and you gave me drink, I was a stranger and you welcomed me, I was naked and you clothed me, I was sick and you visited me, I was in prison and you came to me... Truly, I say to you, as you did it to one of the least of these my brethren, you did it to me.

Matthew 25: 35-36, 40

*M*ichael was sitting on the couch reading as I entered the living room. He looked up from his book and asked, "Dad, could you get me a glass of soda?"

"Sure, Mike," I said as I entered the kitchen. Roe, Michael's mother, called out from the dining room and said, "Chris, Michael is perfectly capable of getting that soda himself."

She was right, of course, but I like getting Michael a drink as he comfortably sits on the couch. I like driving Karen to the high school, to her friends' house, to the movies, the mall, the spa, the baby-sitting jobs, the swim parties. I like washing David's car, carrying his laundry to his room, driving him to college, painting his bedroom, buying him lunch. I like playing Scrabble with Michael, helping him with his train set, pulling him on the motorboat so that he can ski, making him dinner, reading to him. A father, it seems to me, is built to say, simply, yes, yes I can help you.

There is that wonderful little saying, "I am third." The first time I saw these words together was on a small plaque hanging in the dining room of Madonna House when I was a little boy. It has been, actually, one of the foundations for my own living.

God first, others second, and self third. It is, perhaps, why I became a teacher. It is why I married. It is why I like being a father. I serve my students. I serve my wife. I serve my children.

When the children were small I could take care of all their needs. Now as they are all nearly adults I tell them that I can no longer solve all their problems, but I promised them that they can always, always come to me for help no matter what the issue is.

I hope someday when Michael is in need, he remembers how happily his father went to the kitchen to get him that cold glass of orange soda.

Fatherhood is responsibility for life: for the life first conceived in the woman's womb and then born, in order that a new man, who is blood of your blood and flesh of your flesh, may be revealed.

Pope John Paul II, Homily, March 19, 1981

It is more difficult to serve one's fellow human beings than to 'serve the poor'. It is easier to embrace the stranger than to love one's own family, with whom one is so deeply involved by a thousand ties, to whom one comes as a servant-giver of so many things.

Catherine Doherty, Grace in Every Season

Honor your sons and your daughters. They deserve this because they are alive, because they are who they are, and this is true from the first moment of their conception.

Pope John Paul II, Letter to Families

We must be a flame in the darkness, a lamp to our neighbor's feet, a place where he can warm himself, a place where he can see the face of God. It is to love, to burn, that we have come together!

Catherine Doherty, People of the Towel and Water

The past is no longer yours; the future is not yet in your power. You have only the present wherein to do good.

St. Alphonsus

Remind me, God, that I am third. First I will honor you, second my neighbor, and third myself. Help me see the difference between being taken advantage of

and being of service to those I love. I take delight in serving my family, and in so doing I take delight in receiving your gifts, Father, the gifts of your love, the gifts of my children's love, the gift of being a part of their lives as a shepherd, as a teacher, as a servant-giver. For this I am grateful. Amen.

Be hidden. Be a light to your neighbor's feet.
Go without fears into the depth of men's hearts.
I shall be with you.

The Little Mandate

Prayer of a Father and His Child

Let us go to the door with our faith, dear one, let us go to the door with our hope. Let us go to the door of God's house, dear one, let us go to the house with charity. As we enter the house of God, dear love, as we enter his house we will praise him. As we enter the house with gladness, love, we will enter the house with our joy. As we walk down the aisle we will bow our heads, little one, as we walk down the aisle we will bow. As we kneel in his house, we shall sing, dear one, as we kneel we shall sing to delight Him. We will come for this visit to tell our Lord, we will come to say we believe, we believe in the fruit of his love, our Lord, we will come to tell bring him the fruit. As he hears us in prayer he will smile, my dear, God will smile because we shall please him. Now come with me, my little one, come with me to the church and let us praise him.

Do <u>you</u> have a story?

You can help our apostolate in our mission to spread the Gospel by sharing your stories with us!

We invite you to send us your personal accounts of true incidents in your own family life that illustrate the living of "The Little Mandate."

Please send your story to:

Madonna House Publications
Attn: Little Mandate Books
2888 Dafoe Rd
Combermere ON   K0J 1L0
Canada

Please be sure to include your return address.

Notes

Acknowledgments

Photo of Christopher de Vinck on cover by Alex Gotfryd.

We would like to express our gratitude to the following publishers for permission to use quotations:

Tan Books and Publishers, Inc., Rockford, IL, for permission to quote from The Voice of the Saints © 1965 by Burns & Oates, London. Reprinted by TAN Books and Publishers, Inc., by arrangement with Burns & Oates Ltd.

Harmony Media, Inc., Gervais, OR, for permission to quote from The Teachings of Pope John Paul II on CD-ROM and The Illustrated Catholic Bible on CD-ROM.

Scripture quotations are taken from:

The New American Bible ©1991, 1986, 1970 by the Confraternity of Christian Doctrine, Washington, D.C., and are used by permission of the copyright owner. All Rights Reserved. No part of the New American Bible may be reproduced in any form without permission in writing from the copyright owner.

The Revised Standard Version of the Bible: Catholic Edition, copyrighted, © 1966, by the Division of Christian Education of the National Council of the Churches of Christ in the United States of America, and are used by permission. All rights reserved.

If you enjoyed *Fathering*, we think you would also like:

Mothering

Becoming the
Heart of the Home

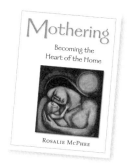

A clarion call to mothers everywhere who are hungering for the truth that is their soul's sustenance, and searching for clarity in the lived-out reality of their vocation to motherhood.

The book includes:
- Becoming a fruitful vessel of love, and 'God's smile' on your children.
- Serving your family with love.
- Becoming an icon of Mary in bringing Jesus to your family.
- Embracing simplicity and prayer.
- Discovering the joy of holy housework and sacred meals.

Mothering features reflections and prayers written by Rosalie McPhee, co-founder of the popular *Nazareth Family Journal* and retreat centre with her late husband, Don. She is mother to five girls and three boys, works with Madonna House Publications, and lives in Combermere, Ontario.

To order, call toll free: 1-888-703-7110

MADONNA HOUSE PUBLICATIONS
COMBERMERE • ONTARIO • CANADA • K0J 1L0

The aim of our publications is to share the Gospel of Jesus Christ with all people from all walks of life.

It is to awaken and deepen in our readers an experience of God's love in the most simple and ordinary facets of everyday life.

It is to make known to our readers how to live the tender, saving life of God in everything they do and for everyone they meet.

Madonna House Publications is a non-profit apostolate of Madonna House within the Catholic Church. Donations allow us to send books to people who cannot afford them but most need them all around the world.

Thank you for your participation in this apostolate!

How to Contact Us

Telephone:	1-613-756-3728
Fax:	1-613-756-0103
Address:	Madonna House Publications
	2888 Dafoe Rd
	Combermere ON K0J 1L0
E-mail:	madonnah@mv.igs.net
Web Site:	www.madonnahouse.org